W9-CLW-629

TRIVIA FUN

Tons of Fun!

By
A. Vandelay

Copyright © 2005 Kidsbooks, LLC
www.kidsbooks.com

All rights reserved including the right
of reproduction in whole or in part in any form.

Manufactured in China

0505-1P

Visit us at **www.kidsbooks.com**

INTRODUCTION

Ever wonder what **capsaicin** is?

Or which ocean has the most islands in it?*

Turn the page for tons of the weirdest, wackiest, and most unbelievable trivia ever! Learn fascinating facts, debunk old myths, and amaze your teachers and classmates with your incredible knowledge! Get ready to learn—and laugh—for hours!

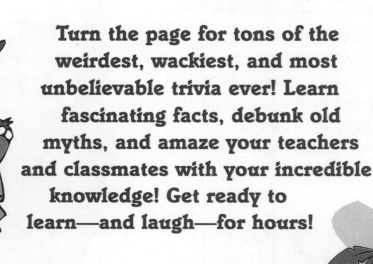

*Capsaicin is the chemical that makes hot peppers hot. The Pacific Ocean has the most islands.

Where in the World?

At the Crater of Diamonds State Park in Murfreesboro, Arkansas, anyone who pays a fee can dig for gemstones and keep whatever is found. It is the only public-use diamond mine in the world.

The city of Pittsburgh, Pennsylvania, has more than 720 bridges.

The world's largest St. Patrick's Day parade is not held in Ireland. It takes place in New York City.

The world's tallest mountain was known as Peak XV until 1865, when it was renamed Mount Everest, in honor of Sir George Everest (1790-1866), a Welsh surveyor.

Water from all five Great Lakes flows into the Atlantic Ocean by a single waterway—the St. Lawrence River and Seaway.

China is the second-largest country in land area. (Russia is the largest.)

Mainland Australia is the only continent with no active volcanoes. (Two active volcanoes can be found on islands that are Australian territory.)

The official state bird of Hawaii is the nene (NAY-nay)—also called the Hawaiian goose.

IT'S SOME BODY!

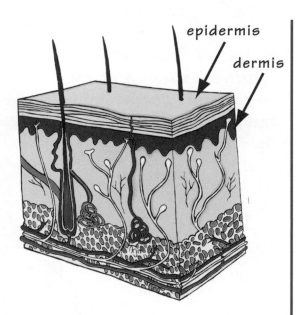

epidermis
dermis

Humans have two layers of skin: the epidermis (outer layer) and the dermis (inner layer).

Blonds have more hair per square inch than redheads and brunettes.

Your lips have no sweat glands.

About 75 percent of the human brain is water.

About 10 percent of the world's population is left-handed.

The average person drinks about 16,000 gallons of water in a lifetime.

The human body must burn 3,500 calories to work off a single pound of fat.

The average human heart, at rest, can pump about 5.3 quarts of blood per minute.

Nature Notes

Water vapor, hydrogen, and dust are all major components of clouds.

Under the best viewing conditions, about 3,000 stars can be seen with the naked eye.

The coconut is the largest plant seed on Earth.

About 20 percent of Earth's surface is covered by warm desert.

The lowest temperature ever recorded in the Sahara Desert was 5 degrees Fahrenheit.

One inch of rain equals 10 inches of snow in water content.

With an average of 106 days of heavy fog a year, Cape Disappointment, Washington, is the foggiest place in the U.S.

Sunflowers really do follow the sun—as buds. When sunflowers are in the bud stage, the buds turn to face the sun as it moves from east to west. After the flowers bloom, however, they face east.

Ninety percent of the world's ice is found in Antarctica.

THIS and THAT

Each year, Americans throw away enough disposable diapers to stretch from here to the moon and back several times.

Men and women started wearing different-style shoes in the 18th century. Before then, men's and women's shoes were the same.

Here is a truly "shocking" fact: A park ranger named Roy C. Sullivan was struck by lightning—and survived—a record seven times between 1942 and 1977.

Most experts believe that the earliest tattoos are the ones found on Egyptian and Nubian mummies dating from about 2000 B.C.

One ounce of gold can be pounded into a thin sheet covering 187 square feet.

Chewing gum while peeling or slicing onions will help keep your eyes from tearing.

The ancient Romans loved luxurious baths. Wealthy men were known to bathe in wine and wealthy women in milk.

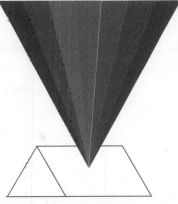

The seven colors in the light spectrum always appear in the same order: red, orange, yellow, green, blue, indigo, and violet. To remember this, imagine someone named Roy G. Biv. Each letter of that name is the first letter of those seven colors, in order.

The Amazing U.S.A.

Q. How long is the term of a U.S. senator?

A. six years

Q. Who was the first American woman to walk in space?

A. Challenger astronaut Kathryn Sullivan, in October 1984

Q. The nickname "Old Glory" refers to what?

A. the U.S. flag

Q. Who was America's first known female soldier?

A. Deborah Sampson (during the American Revolution)

Q. About how many Native Americans live in the U.S. today?

A. two million (About one third of them live on reservations.)

Q. What was the first colony in North America to outlaw slavery?

A. Rhode Island (on May 18, 1652)

Q. Robert E. Lee was the third-ranking officer in the Confederate Army. Who was the first?

A. Samuel Cooper

Q. After the original 13 colonies, what was the next state to enter the Union?

A. Vermont (on March 4, 1791)

Q. Which state has a law on its books requiring every citizen to take a bath at least once a year?

A. Kentucky

SPORTS STUFF

Most wooden baseball bats are made from the wood of ash trees.

The NFL's all-time leading rusher is Emmitt Smith. By the end of the 2004 season, he had 18,355 career yards.

Tug-of-war was once an Olympic event.

The first World Cup soccer tournament was held in 1930. Uruguay's team defeated Argentina's 4–2.

The original name of the game of hockey was hurley.

A panel of experts named Jack Nicklaus the male Golfer of the Century for the 20th century and Mickey Wright the female Golfer of the Century.

Frank Robinson was the first baseball player to win the Most Valuable Player award in both major leagues. He was named the National League's MVP in 1961, when he was with the Cincinnati Reds. The American League named him MVP in 1966, when he was playing for the Baltimore Orioles.

The first TV broadcast of a major-league baseball game took place on August 26, 1939. The game was between the Brooklyn Dodgers and the Cincinnati Reds. (A college baseball game, between Columbia and Princeton universities, was broadcast on May 10, 1939.)

Joe Montana, quarterback of the San Francisco 49ers, was the first football player to win the Super Bowl MVP award three times—in 1982, 1985, and 1990.

ANIMAL ANTICS

A pigeon's bones weigh less than its feathers.

With a record weight of more than 2,000 pounds, the leatherback sea turtle is the world's largest turtle.

Most spiders have eight eyes, but some have six, or four, or fewer.

Lions once roamed wild in North America, but they disappeared from the North American continent about 10,000 years ago.

Snakes do not have ears. They "hear" by sensing vibrations through the jawbone, which sends signals through connecting bones to the inner ear and brain.

An adult male flamingo is three to five feet tall. Female flamingos are slightly shorter.

The mako shark has been clocked at a speed of 43 miles per hour, making it the fastest swimmer of all sharks.

There are about 170,000 different kinds of butterflies and moths.

The ocean sunfish (also called the mola or the headfish) produces more eggs at one time than any other kind of fish—up to 300,000,000.

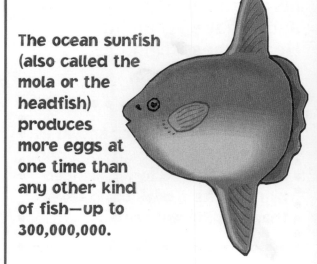

TV, Movies, Music, & More

In 1953, an unknown singer named Elvis Presley paid $3.98 to record two songs to his mother: "My Happiness" and "That's When Your Heartaches Begin."

Theodor Geisel, better known as Dr. Seuss, wrote *Green Eggs and Ham* after an editor challenged him to write a book using fewer than 50 different words.

There are 64 squares on a chessboard.

It is possible to deal 2,598,960 different five-card poker hands from a 52-card deck.

Bram Stoker set his famous novel *Dracula* in Transylvania—a real place in Europe that he had never visited.

Snoopy, the famous comic-strip beagle, was born at the Daisy Hill Puppy Farm.

A CAST OF THOUSANDS

The Academy Award®-winning movie *Gandhi*, directed by Richard Attenborough, used hundreds of thousands of extras—the most ever used in a film. More than 300,000 extras appear in the funeral scene alone.

Author L. Frank Baum named Oz after a filing-cabinet drawer in his office. One was labeled "A–N"; the other, "O–Z."

Arthur Wynne, an English journalist, created the first crossword puzzle known to be published. His puzzle ran in the *New York World* newspaper on December 21, 1913.

Science Fair

The largest constellation in the sky is Hydra, also known as the Water Snake, the Sea Serpent, or the Water Monster.

Nylon was the first completely synthetic material ever made. On "N" Day—May 15, 1940—nylon's inventor, DuPont, began selling stockings made with nylon, and sold 780,000 pairs in one day.

In areas that are sunny most of the year, solar energy—collected by special panels—can be an efficient, nonpolluting energy source.

If the diameter of Earth were 10 percent smaller, all life would freeze.

Galileo Galilei invented the thermometer to measure air temperature, in about 1592.

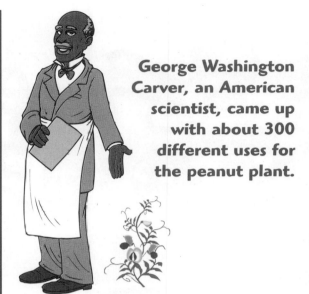

George Washington Carver, an American scientist, came up with about 300 different uses for the peanut plant.

Earth orbits the sun at about 66,700 miles per hour.

The technique of growing plants without soil is called hydroponics.

An accidental error in a computer program is called a *bug*. The term originated in 1945, when a malfunctioning computer at Harvard University was found to have a moth in one of its circuits.

Famous Folks

Q. Who, in 1896, told newspaper reporters this now-famous statement: "The report of my death has been greatly exaggerated"?

A. Mark Twain, the famous author, responding to rumors that he had died

Q. Jane Goodall is famous for studying what kind of animals?

A. chimpanzees

Q. The captain of the British ship *Endeavour* successfully navigated the Great Barrier Reef off the coast of Australia—one of the world's most challenging sea courses. What was his name?

A. James Cook (1728-1779)

Q. Helen Keller could not see, hear, or speak. What was the name of the teacher who helped her overcome her disabilities?

A. Anne Sullivan

Q. Who said, "Genius is one percent inspiration, ninety-nine percent perspiration"?

A. Thomas Alva Edison, the famous inventor

Q. Who wrote: "In spite of everything, I still believe that people are good at heart"?

A. Anne Frank (in The Diary of Anne Frank)

Q. Who said, "No one can make you feel inferior without your consent"?

A. Eleanor Roosevelt

Q. What did Charles Dickens, Thomas Alva Edison, and Mark Twain have in common?

A. None of them finished elementary school.

ANYONE HUNGRY?

In 1597, an English herbalist named John Gerard published *The Herball*—the first known catalogue of plants. It included a then-popular belief: that tomatoes are poisonous. Italians, Arabs, and Spaniards ate tomatoes, but few English or Americans did so until the early 19th century.

Natural vanilla flavoring comes from orchids. (Vanilla beans are the unripe fruit of certain types of tropical orchid plants.)

Pizza is the most popular food in the U.S.

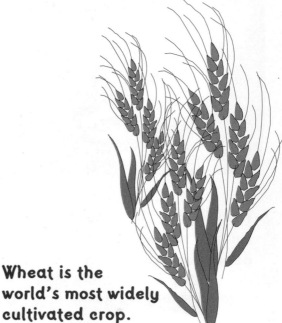

Wheat is the world's most widely cultivated crop.

Corn is grown on every continent of the world except Antarctica.

Why wash dishes? A Taiwanese inventor has come up with plates and bowls made of oatmeal. After finishing your meal, you can eat the plate—or boil it into a paste to feed pets or farm animals!

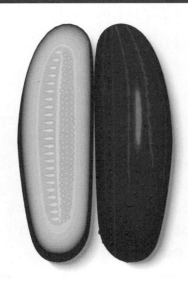

A cucumber is 96 percent water.

Monks in Germany created the pretzel in 610 A.D. Its shape was meant to represent a child's arms folded in prayer.

Americans eat a lot of chocolate—more than 11 pounds per person per year. But the U.S. is only 11th in worldwide chocolate consumption. Number one is Switzerland: more than 22 pounds per person a year!

WAY BACK WHEN

In 1744, Benjamin Franklin issued the first mail-order catalogue in the U.S.—to sell books.

The circus as we know it today came into being during the mid-1700s.

In 1908, five years after the famous first flight at Kitty Hawk, North Carolina, Wilbur Wright made his longest flight. He stayed aloft for more than 2 hours and traveled 77 miles.

Before Michelangelo created his famous paintings on the ceiling of the Vatican's Sistine Chapel, the ceiling was painted with golden stars on a blue sky.

The first shots of the Civil War were fired on April 12, 1861, at Fort Sumter, in the harbor of Charleston, South Carolina.

About one million people—one eighth of the population—died from starvation when Ireland's potato crop failed in 1845-1850.

The first time a U.S. street was paved with asphalt was in 1870 in Newark, New Jersey.

King Kullen, the world's first supermarket, opened in the U.S. in 1930.

Alexandre-Gustave Eiffel, the man who designed Paris's Eiffel Tower, also helped build another world-famous structure: the Statue of Liberty. Frédéric-Auguste Bartholdi was the Statue's sculptor, but Eiffel helped design the framework that supports it.

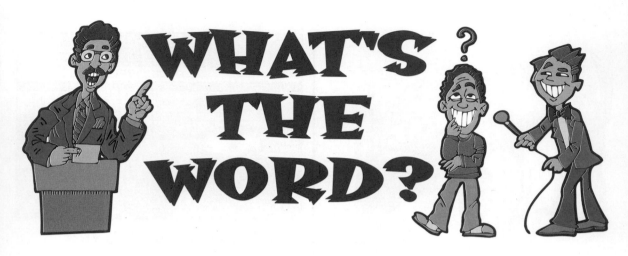

WHAT'S THE WORD?

A group of crows
is called a *murder*.

Every letter of the alphabet
appears at least once in this
sentence: *The quick brown fox
jumps over the lazy dog.*

The acronym *radar* stands for
"**ra**dio **d**etecting **a**nd **r**anging."

Signs with the warning CAVE
CANEM were used by ancient
Romans. It means "Beware
the dog!"

It took Noah Webster about 17 years to compile the first American dictionary, the *American Dictionary of the English Language*. (He started it in 1807 and finished it in 1824–1825.)

The name *Jeep* came from the letters *GP*. At first, they were a manufacturer's abbreviation: *G* for government, *P* for a certain type of reconnaissance car. Later, they were short for "general purpose."

A *horologist* is not someone who writes or reads horoscopes. It is a person who makes or repairs clocks. (The term comes from the Greek word *hora,* meaning "hour" or "season."

A xenophobe (ZEH-nuh-fobe) is someone who fears foreigners. The term comes from the Greek words *xenos*, meaning "stranger," and *phobos*, meaning "fear.")

Where in the World?

Mount Aconcagua *(ah-kone-KAH-gwah)*, in Argentina, is the highest point in the Western Hemisphere. It rises 22,834 feet above sea level.

Until railroads made it possible to travel long distances in a short time, every area set its own standard time. Time zones were invented to help travelers avoid schedule problems.

More than 400 cities in the world have a population of more than 1 million.

Of all the world's continents, South America has the greatest variety of plants and animals.

There are more islands in the Pacific Ocean—about 25,000—than in all the other oceans combined.

The continent of Africa has 53 independent countries.

In the English language, only five of the world's countries have one-syllable names: Chad, France, Greece, Laos (in one of its pronunciations), and Spain.

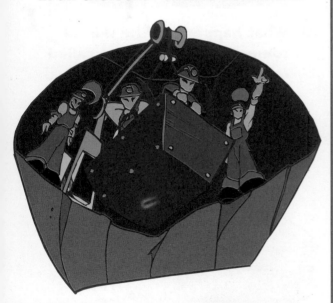

Utah is home to the biggest man-made hole in the U.S., and one of the biggest on Earth: a copper mine near the village of Bingham Canyon.

In Matanchen Bay, Mexico, the waves are so long that a surfer can ride a single wave for more than 5,000 feet—almost a mile!

IT'S SOME BODY!

Q. Many people have a malady called *furfur*. What is it?

A. dandruff

Q. What happens to the skin of someone with a disease called *ichthyosis* (ik-thee-OH-sis)?

A. It becomes dry and scaly.

Q. Where did the expression "goose pimples" come from?

A. from how a goose's skin looks when its feathers are plucked (also called goose bumps or gooseflesh)

Q. About how many times does the average human take a breath during a 24-hour period?

A. 24,000

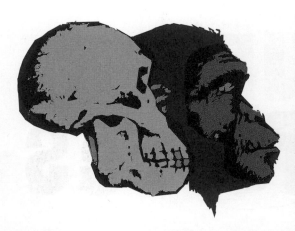

Q. **Was the brain of a Neanderthal larger or smaller than ours?**

A. larger

Q. **How long does it take for blood to make a complete circuit of the human body?**

A. under a minute

Q. **If you lose the sight in one eye, how much of your vision do you lose?**

A. about one fifth (but all of your depth perception)

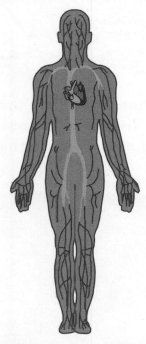

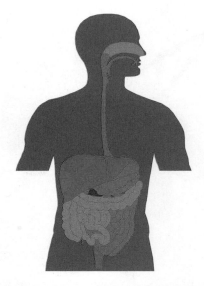

Q. **About how long is the small intestine in an adult human?**

A. 22 to 25 feet long

Q. **How many miles of blood vessels, on average, are in the human body?**

A. about 100,000 miles for an adult; about 60,000 miles for a child

Nature Notes

More water flows from the Amazon River into the ocean than from any other river in the world.

A single galaxy can contain hundreds of billions of stars.

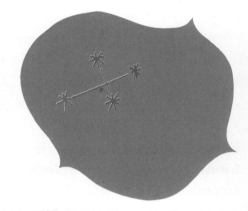

The smallest constellation is the Southern Cross—also called Crux.

An oak tree must be at least 20 years old before it can produce acorns.

The most destructive volcanic eruption in the history of the United States was the eruption of Mount St. Helens, in Washington, in May 1980.

A lunar month is 29.53 days—the length of time it takes from one new moon to the next (also called lunation).

Flowering plants first appeared during the Cretaceous Period (145 to 65 million years ago).

The *cumulonimbus (KYOOM-yuh-loh-NIM-bus)* is the tallest type of cloud. It can tower from near the ground to as high as 60,000 feet—more than twice the height of Mount Everest.

The world's tallest grass, bamboo, can grow to a height of 130 feet.

ANIMAL ANTICS

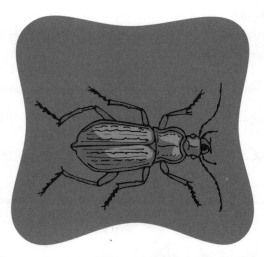

A cockroach can live about a week without its head. It dies of thirst, because it can't drink water.

The capybara, which lives in Central and South America, is the world's largest rodent. It can grow to 4 feet in length and weigh 100 pounds.

Cats do not chew food the same way humans do. They use their teeth to cut through or tear up food, then they swallow it in large chunks.

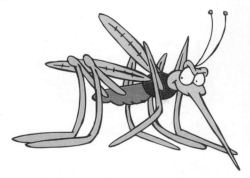

Worldwide, there are about 2,500 different mosquito species. About 150 of them live in the U.S.

The honeybee communicates by doing distinctive dances.

The sun bear, found in southeast Asia, is the smallest type of bear. The largest is the Kodiak bear, a type of brown bear. It is the largest living land carnivore.

There are more than 20,000 species of fish.

The aardvark, whose name in the Afrikaans language means "earth pig," feeds mostly on ants and termites.

An adult dog has 42 teeth.

THIS and THAT

One drop per second from a leaky faucet will waste 2,700 gallons of water in a year.

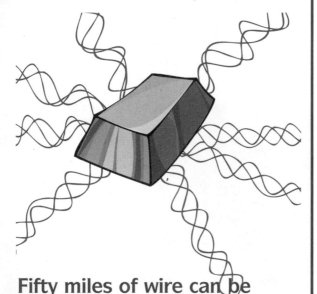

Fifty miles of wire can be made from one ounce of gold.

Royalties from Irving Berlin's song "God Bless America" go to the Boy and Girl Scouts of America.

The Smithsonian Institution, in Washington, D.C., is the largest museum complex in the world. It has 16 separate museums and the National Zoo, as well as various research centers.

The sound of human snoring can get close to 90 decibels—about as loud as a lawn mower or chain saw.

King Arthur's sword had a name: Excalibur.

If you lie on your back and slowly raise your legs, you won't sink in quicksand.

An old Texas almanac advised that tea made by boiling an old shoe was a good cure for lumbago (backache).

In skywriting, the average letter is 1,320 feet (quarter-mile) high, and the plume of smoke is about 75 feet wide.

The Amazing U.S.A.

The first U.S. Minimum Wage Law was passed in 1938. At that time, the minimum wage was 25¢ an hour.

If the heads on Mount Rushmore had bodies, the statues would be about 500 feet tall—about as tall as a 50-story skyscraper.

Americans use about 50,000 pounds of toothpaste per day.

The first female governor in the U.S. was Nellie Tayloe Ross. In 1924, she was elected in place of her husband, Governor William Bradford Ross of Wyoming, who died while running for reelection.

EVERYONE KNOWS THAT I'M WORTH TEN CENTS!

A dime is the only U.S. coin that does not say how many cents it is worth.

Big Bend National Park, in southwestern Texas, is the only national park that runs along part of the U.S.–Mexico border. For a little more than 100 miles, it forms the U.S. side of the Rio Grande, the official border between the U.S. and Mexico.

Benjamin Franklin was unhappy with the choice of the bald eagle as the symbol of the United States. He wanted it to be the wild turkey.

The cadet colors at the U.S. Military Academy at West Point, New York, are black, gray, and gold. The colors represent the components of gunpowder: charcoal (black), potassium nitrate (gray), and sulfur (gold).

The official name of the Statue of Liberty is *Liberty Enlightening the World*.

SPORTS STUFF

Baseball manager Casey Stengel once told a player, "Kid, you're too small. You ought to go out and shine shoes." That "kid," Phil Rizzuto, stuck with baseball. He became a star shortstop for the New York Yankees, and was inducted into the Baseball Hall of Fame in 1994.

Surfing was invented hundreds of years ago by Polynesians.

ONE, TWO, THREE . . .

There are 324 to 492 dimples on a modern golf ball.

In 1986, Greg LeMond became the first non-European bicyclist—and first American—to win the 2,235-mile-long race called the Tour de France. (He also won it in 1989 and 1990.)

An official baseball weighs between 5 and 5.25 ounces.

Rickey Henderson holds the career record in pro baseball for stolen bases.

The first Wimbledon tennis tournament was held at Merton, England, in 1877.

The Harlem Globetrotters, a famous basketball team that excels in comedy as well as ball-handling skills, has been entertaining audiences since 1927.

Think it is easy for a golfer to get a hole in one? Think again: The odds are about 1 in 25,000!

TV, Movies, Music, & More

Q. In the classic Bugs Bunny cartoon *Rabbit Hood,* the Sheriff of Nottingham catches Bugs doing what?

A. taking carrots from the king's garden

Q. What was the motto of the Three Musketeers?

A. "All for one and one for all!"

Q. What fictional character is known as the "boy who wouldn't grow up"?

A. Peter Pan, from a 1904 play by James M. Barrie called *Peter Pan, the Boy Who Wouldn't Grow Up*

Q. What type of dragon did Viktor Krum face in book four of the Harry Potter series?

A. a Chinese Fireball (in *Harry Potter and the Goblet of Fire* by J. K. Rowling)

Q. Can you name all the dwarfs in the movie *Snow White and the Seven Dwarfs*?

A. Bashful, Doc, Dopey, Grumpy, Happy, Sleepy, and Sneezy

Q. Match the superhero with his secret identity:

1. Barry Allen, police scientist
2. Bruce Banner, scientist
3. Hal Jordan, test pilot
4. Matt Murdock, lawyer

a. Daredevil

b. The Flash

c. The Green Lantern

d. The Incredible Hulk

A. 1–b; 2–d; 3–c; 4–a

Q. Street names from a real place were used in the original version of the Monopoly board game. What is the city?

A. Atlantic City, New Jersey

Q. In *The Wizard of Oz*, who wanted Dorothy's shoes?

A. the Wicked Witch of the West

Q. In the Harry Potter books, what is the animal shop in Diagon Alley called?

A. Magical Menagerie

Science Fair

It takes a space probe about 7 to 10 months to get to Mars.

In 1962, U.S. astronaut John Glenn became the first person to eat in space. He ate applesauce and pureed beef squeezed from tubes. (Glenn's meal helped scientists learn how humans were affected by weightlessness in space.)

The Holland Tunnel was the world's first long, mechanically ventilated underwater tunnel for motor vehicles. Opened in 1927, it connects New York and New Jersey under the Hudson River and is still in use.

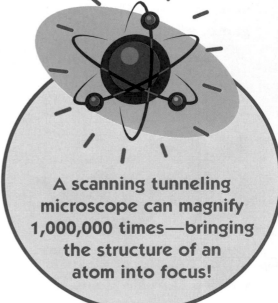

A scanning tunneling microscope can magnify 1,000,000 times—bringing the structure of an atom into focus!

The Beaufort scale is used to measure the speed of wind. It was named for the man who devised it, Sir Francis Beaufort (pronounced *BOH-furt*).

A *paleontologist* is a scientist who studies fossils.

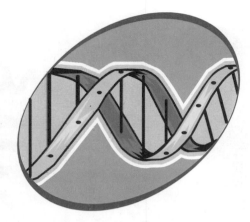

Scientists studying the DNA of a 9,000-year-old skeleton found in England discovered that the skeleton had a living descendant—a local schoolteacher!

If you could drive from Earth to the sun at a speed of 60 miles per hour, it would take about 177 years to get there.

Famous Folks

Vincent van Gogh (1853-1890) created more than 800 oil paintings and 700 drawings. Today, one of his paintings may sell for millions of dollars. During his lifetime, however, he was poverty stricken and sold only one painting.

John D. Rockefeller built the first modern industrial empire. Through his Standard Oil Company, Rockefeller controlled nearly all of the production, processing, and marketing of oil in the U.S.

Samuel Langhorne Clemens was the real name of Mark Twain, creator of Tom Sawyer and Huckleberry Finn. Clemens took his pen name from a riverboat term, *mark twain*, which means "two fathoms deep" (a depth of about 12 feet).

In 1879, Belva Ann Lockwood became the first woman to argue a case before the U.S. Supreme Court.

Alexander Graham Bell's mother and wife were both unable to use his famous invention, the telephone. They were deaf.

A frontierswoman who was born Martha Jane Cannary was buried in South Dakota with a gun in each hand. She also was known by her married name, Martha Jane Burke. However, she was much more famous by another name: Calamity Jane.

The Boston Tea Party of 1773, one of the most famous protests in American history, was organized by Samuel Adams. (He was second cousin to John Adams, a founding father and the second president of the U.S.)

ANYONE HUNGRY?

A pineapple is a fruit that starts out as lavender-colored flowers. The flowers fuse, developing into the pineapple fruit.

The chemical in chili peppers that makes them hot is called capsaicin.

Garlic belongs to the lily family of plants (Liliaceae).

About 60 percent of all sandwiches eaten in the U.S. are hamburgers.

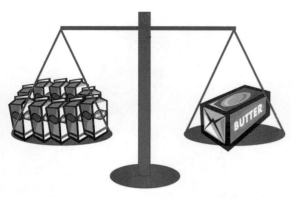

About 10 quarts of milk are needed to make one pound of butter.

About 30,000 peanut-butter sandwiches can be made from one acre of peanuts.

About 70 percent of all the popcorn consumed in the U.S. is eaten in the home.

Americans eat more than 100 acres of pizza each day.

Potato chips were originally called Saratoga chips.

WAY BACK WHEN

Christopher Columbus made four expeditions to the New World.

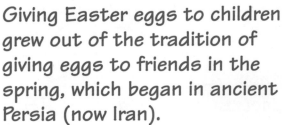

Giving Easter eggs to children grew out of the tradition of giving eggs to friends in the spring, which began in ancient Persia (now Iran).

In ancient Greece, one of the most popular male fashions was wearing a beard—fake beards as well as real ones.

On September 22, 1776, just before being hanged as a spy, 21-year-old Nathan Hale spoke these now-famous words: "I only regret that I have but one life to lose for my country." Hale, a schoolteacher, had joined the American army during the American Revolution.

The first hard candies, produced to relieve coughing, were made in Egypt, around 1000 B.C.

An early form of the bicycle, first seen in the 18th century, was known as a "dandy horse."

At one point in history, people in Scotland refused to eat potatoes, because they were not mentioned in the Bible.

The coffee plant originated in what today is Ethiopia. Using the beans to make a drink began in Arabia in the 15th century.

According to legend, twins named Romulus and Remus founded the city of Rome, Italy. As babies, they were swept down the Tiber River, but landed safely. A wolf and a woodpecker took care of them until a herdsman found them.

ANIMAL ANTICS

Q. Are all lobsters red?

A. Only those that have been cooked in hot water. In nature, lobsters are many colors, including blue, gray, greenish-brown, and yellow—but never red.

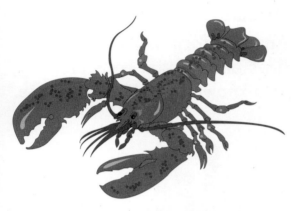

Q. At what age does a filly become a mare?

A. four years

Q. What is a Gila monster?

A. a type of lizard (pronounced HEE-luh) It is one of only two lizard species that are poisonous. The other is the Mexican beaded lizard

Q. What is a group of kangaroos called?

A. a troop (other collective nouns for kangaroos: herd and mob)

Q. In which direction does a fly take off from a horizontal surface?

A. upward and backward (Now you know which way to aim the flyswatter!)

Q. What type of whale has a head that is 20 feet long, 10 feet high, and 7 feet wide?

A. the sperm whale

Q. How many different species of penguins are there?

A. 17

Q. How many living species of bears are there?

A. eight: the Asiatic black bear, the American black bear, the brown bear, the giant panda, the polar bear, the sloth bear, the spectacled bear, and the sun bear

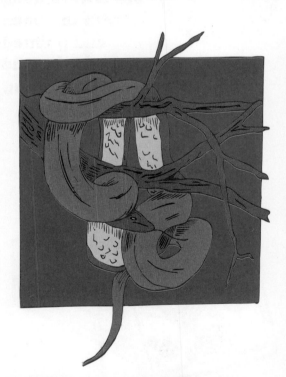

Q. What type of snake weighs more than any other?

A. the anaconda (It can weigh more than 1,100 pounds.)

THiS and THAT

Horseshoes, a common symbol of good luck, are always hung with the open end pointed upward—so that the good luck will not drain out.

Before making a fortune in computer games, Nintendo manufactured playing cards.

The world's largest collection of baseball cards is not at the National Baseball Hall of Fame, but at the Metropolitan Museum of Art in New York City. The museum has thousands of cards in its collection, too many to show at once. A rotating exhibit shows different cards, 16 sets at a time.

48B98D12F

In Japan, most cars are sold by door-to-door salespersons who visit the homes of potential customers.

The "black boxes" that record flight data on commercial airplanes are not black. They are orange.

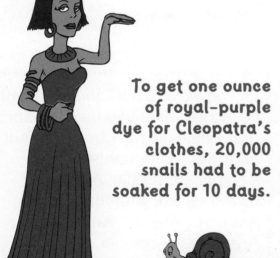

To get one ounce of royal-purple dye for Cleopatra's clothes, 20,000 snails had to be soaked for 10 days.

AUGUST

1	2	3	4	5	6	7
8	9	10	11	12	13	14
15	16	17	18	19	20	21
22	23	24	25	26	27	28
29	30	31				

A Friday the 13th will occur in any month in which the first day is a Sunday.

Rubber toy balloons were introduced in 1825. Before then, they were made of animal bladders or intestines filled with water or air.

48B98D12F

Where in the World?

China has more land frontiers than any other country. It borders 14 independent countries: Afghanistan, Bhutan, India, Kazakhstan, Kyrgyzstan, Laos, Mongolia, Myanmar (Burma), Nepal, North Korea, Pakistan, Russia, Tajikistan, and Vietnam.

The Caspian Sea is the largest inland body of water in the world. It lies in Central Asia, and covers 149,200 square miles of land—an area larger than Germany.

Not counting the continent of Australia, Greenland is the largest island on Earth.

Of the world's 193 independent countries, only two have a name that begins with *A* but does not end with *A*: Afghanistan and Azerbaijan. (Other *A*-starting countries are Albania, Algeria, Andorra, Angola, Antigua, Argentina, Armenia, Australia, and Austria.)

The city of Venice, Italy, is made up of 118 small islands, connected by about 150 canals and 400 bridges.

The smallest 21 U.S. states would fit into the land area of Alaska.

The Canary Islands were not named after birds. The name is from *canes (KAH-nez),* the Latin word for "dogs."

The longest suspension bridge in the world is Akashi Kaikyo Bridge in Japan. It has a main span of 6,570 feet. (That is 1.24 miles!)

IT'S SOME BODY!

HMMM . . . WHERE IS IT?

The smallest bone in your body is the stapes (STAY-peez), also called the stirrup. It is in your ear.

If you could spread out the surface of the inside of your lungs, it would be the size of a tennis court.

The skin of an adult human weighs five to eight pounds.

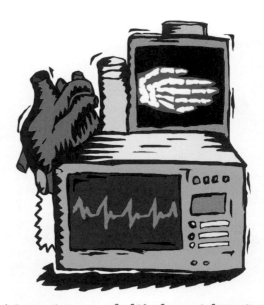

At rest, an adult's heart beats about 72 times per minute. That is 4,320 beats an hour—103,680 beats a day—and more than 37 million beats in a year!

There are 26 bones in each human foot. This means that about one quarter of all the bones in your body are in your feet! There are even more in your hands— 27 bones each.

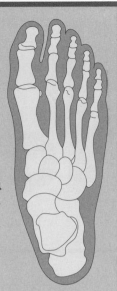

Like fingerprints, every person's tongue print is unique.

Arteries and veins are both blood vessels. So what is the difference? *Arteries* carry oxygen-rich blood *from* the heart through the body. *Veins* carry the depleted blood *to* the heart for more oxygen.

CRUNCHY O's

In the U.S., the average person eats about 17 pounds of cereal per year.

The human mouth produces one quarter to one half gallon of saliva each day.

Nature Notes

The rings around the planet Saturn are composed of chunks of rock and ice.

Two elements, together, comprise 98 percent of all known matter in the universe: hydrogen (about 73 percent) and helium (about 25 percent).

There are about 1,650 different species of cactus plants.

Lightning strikes Earth about 8.6 million times a day.

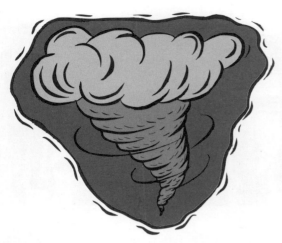

Most tornadoes on Earth occur in central/southeastern U.S.

The greatest known deposit of copper in the world is in Chile, in the Andes Mountains.

Pecans come from hickory trees. The pecan tree is one of several species of hickory. Hickory trees belong to the same family as walnuts, but the nuts of the two trees are quite different.

Old Faithful, in Yellowstone National Park, is the most famous geyser in North America.

A supernova is the explosion of a very large, collapsing star.

The Amazing U.S.A.

The U.S. Congress officially recognized "Uncle Sam" as a national symbol in 1961. The term *Uncle Sam* as a nickname for the United States has been around a long time. It was first used during the War of 1812.

Petrified wood is the official state gem of Washington.

Jousting has been the official sport of Maryland since 1962.

Have you ever noticed the two Latin mottoes on the back of a U.S. dollar bill? *ANNUIT CŒPTIS* means "He [God] has favored our undertakings." *NOVUS ORDO SECLORUM* means "A new order of the ages."

"Little red schoolhouses" were painted red because red paint was the cheapest available.

The Smithsonian Institution in Washington, D.C., was founded as a gift from James Smithson—an English scientist who had never set foot in the U.S.!

The Great Seal of the United States was officially adopted by the Continental Congress in 1782. The Great Seal is still used today. Over the centuries, only minor changes have been made to the original design.

More American soldiers lost their lives during the Civil War than in any other war in which U.S. troops have fought. More than 617,500 soldiers were killed—about 359,500 from the North and about 258,000 from the South.

The state with the largest proven crude-oil reserves is Texas (nearly five million barrels).

SPORTS STUFF

Q. How many consecutive strikes does it take to bowl a perfect game?

A. 12 (a score of 300)

Q. Which kind of sporting equipment outsells baseballs, basketballs, and footballs combined?

A. Frisbees

Q. In rodeo-competition bull riding, how long must the rider hang on?

A. eight seconds

Q. Cy Young holds the record for most games won by a major-league pitcher: 511. What was his real name?

A. Denton True Young (Cy was short for "cyclone," because of the speed of his fastball.)

Q. What game requires the largest playing field?

A. polo (Those ponies need a lot of room to run! A polo field is 300 yards long and 160 yards wide.)

Q. In baseball, the distance between bases is 90 feet. What is the size of first, second, and third bases?

A. 15" x 15" (and 3" deep)

Q. A feathery was an item used in which sport in the 17th century?

A. golf (A feathery was a golf ball made from boiled feathers that were squeezed into a stitched-leather cover.)

Q. Which heavyweight boxing champ was once knocked out of the ring in the first round, yet came back to win in the second round?

A. Jack Dempsey (against Luis Angel Firpo on September 14, 1923)

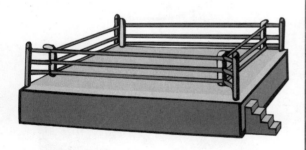

Q. Who was the only pro basketball player to score 100 points in a single regulation game?

A. Wilt Chamberlain on March 2, 1962, vs. the New York Knicks (Chamberlain's Philadelphia Warriors won, 169-147.)

ANIMAL ANTICS

The tiny red-billed quelea, which is native to East Africa, has the greatest population of any living bird. More than four million can live in an area smaller than 125 acres.

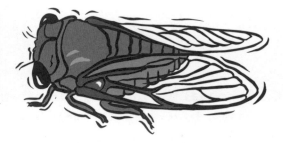

The call of the world's loudest insect, the African cicada, can be as loud as 106.7 decibels—about the same loudness as a car horn.

Although the wolf spider looks pretty nasty, its bite is not harmful to humans.

The emu, the kiwi, the ostrich, and the penguin are all birds that cannot fly.

A cat has a better memory than a dog.

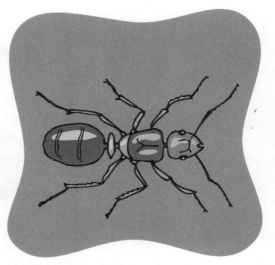

The animal with the largest brain in proportion to its size is the ant.

The bumblebee bat, weighing less than a penny, is the smallest mammal in the world.

A baby blue whale can drink about 44 gallons of milk a day and gain 7 pounds an hour!

A camel is fully mature at six to eight years of age.

TV, Movies, Music, & More

Gene Autry was a famous "singing cowboy" of movies and one-time owner of the Texas Rangers baseball team. He has another claim to fame: In 1948, he recorded "Rudolph the Red-nosed Reindeer," a song that remains an all-time hit.

The final episode of the series *M*A*S*H* holds the record for largest audience rating in TV history. More than 105.4 million viewers in 50.15 million homes—about 77 percent of all viewers—tuned in to watch that program on February 28, 1983.

The planet in *The Planet of the Apes*, a popular sci-fi book, was Earth. (The book, by Pierre Boulle, was the basis of several movies.)

The first thing that Clark Kent takes off when changing into Superman is his eyeglasses.

Early prints of the 1931 film *Frankenstein* had some scenes tinted green, the "color of fear." Audiences found them so horrible that they were pulled from theaters and replaced by prints that were all black and white.

In *The Lord of the Rings*, Gollum's real name is Smeagol.

The Adventures of Tom Sawyer, by Mark Twain, was the first manuscript produced on a typewriter.

There are 100 letter tiles in a Scrabble crossword game.

Film star Charlie Chaplin once lost a Charlie Chaplin look-alike contest.

Science Fair

A *hygrometer* is an instrument that measures the relative humidity of air. You don't need special equipment, though—human hair is a natural hygrometer. Hair tends to curl as moisture in the air increases, and to straighten in dry conditions.

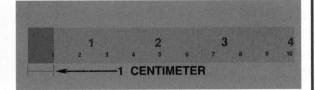

1 CENTIMETER

Most countries today use the *metric* system of measurement, which includes meters for distance and liters for volume. The U.S. uses a different system, which includes miles, yards, and feet for distance, and quarts and gallons for volume. It is known as the *imperial* system.

In 1839, Thedor Schwann, a German biologist, published *Microscopic Researches Into Accordance in the Structure and Growth of Animals and Plants*. Schwann's careful studies of plant and animal life helped convince other scientists of an idea that we now take for granted—that cells are the basic unit of all animal life.

In 1997, researchers in Scotland performed the first successful cloning of an adult mammal. A lamb known as Dolly was created from a single cell taken from a sheep. The lamb was an exact genetic copy of the sheep.

Karl Benz, a German engineer, built the first automobile powered by an internal-combustion engine. His three-wheel vehicle had its first successful test drive in 1885.

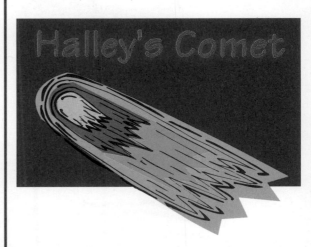

A *pathologist* is a scientist who studies diseases—their causes, how they develop and progress, and their effects on the body. Some pathologists specialize in problems other than disease. For instance, a *speech pathologist* studies stuttering and other speech problems. A *forensic pathologist* looks for a cause of death.

In 1705, astronomer Edmond Halley said that large comets seen in 1531, 1607, and 1682 were all the *same* comet—and that it would return in 1758. It did! Records of the comet's visits go back as far as 240 B.C. Its last visit was in 1985-1986. It next will be visible from Earth in 2061.

PRESIDENTS ON PARADE

"Good to the last drop," a phrase that is still used in ads for a brand of coffee, was coined by President Theodore Roosevelt.

The phrase "of the people, by the people, and for the people" is from the Gettysburg Address, a speech made by President Abraham Lincoln on November 19, 1863.

Franklin D. Roosevelt was the only person elected president four times, and he served longer than any other U.S. president (1933-1945). That won't happen again. In 1955, the Constitution was changed, limiting presidents to two terms.

When George Washington was president, slaves made up 20 percent of the U.S. population. At the time, however, census takers counted each slave as three fifths of a person.

Woodrow Wilson was the first U.S. president to visit Europe while in office. He went there in December 1918 to take part in the Paris Peace Conference.

Richard M. Nixon was the first U.S. president to place a telephone call to the moon. On July 20, 1969, he spoke with astronauts Neil Armstrong and Edwin "Buzz" Aldrin—the first people to set foot on Earth's closest neighbor.

Eleven-year-old Grace Bedell wrote a letter to Abraham Lincoln, suggesting that he would get more votes if he grew a beard.

President Thomas Jefferson is credited with introducing waffles and macaroni to the U.S. He found out how to make macaroni while touring Italy, and took a waffle iron home to Virginia after tasting waffles in the Netherlands.

THIS and THAT

Q. What was the first automobile mass-produced in the U.S.?

A. The Oldsmobile, manufactured by Ransome Eli Olds in 1901. (About 12 years later, Henry Ford invented an improved assembly-line process.)

Q. What is the main use, by humans, of squirrel hairs?

A. They are used to make camel-hair paintbrushes. The brushes are also made with goat, pony, and ox hair, but not with hair from camels.

Q. What is the most common surname in the world?

A. Chang

Q. What company was the first to mass-market rubber-soled shoes as canvas-topped sneakers?

A. Keds, in 1917

48B98D12F

Q. Where does the saying "Don't count your chickens before they are hatched" come from?

A. an Aesop's fable

Q. During what century is Robin Hood said to have robbed from the rich and given to the poor?

A. the 12th century

Q. How many dollar bills, laid lengthwise end to end, would it take to encircle Earth at the equator?

A. 256,964,529 dollar bills (Earth's circumference at equator: 24,901.55 miles; a dollar bill's length: 6.14 inches)

Q. Whose heart beats faster: an adult human or an elephant?

A. an adult human (adult human's heart: 70 to 80 beats per minute; elephant's heart: about 25 beats per minute)

48B98D12F

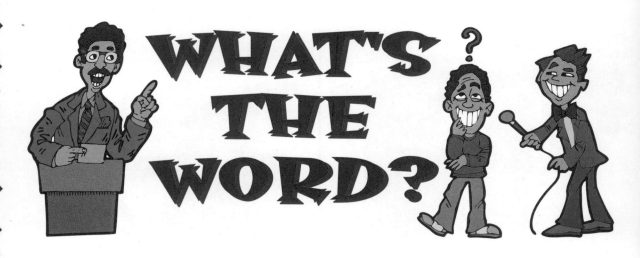

WHAT'S THE WORD?

The saying "Love makes the world go round" comes from the Middle Ages. According to religious teachings of that time, love was what set the universe in motion.

The Chinese characters for the word *gunpowder* translate as "fire medicine."

The first person to use the word *nerd* was Dr. Seuss, in his 1950 book *If I Ran the Zoo.*

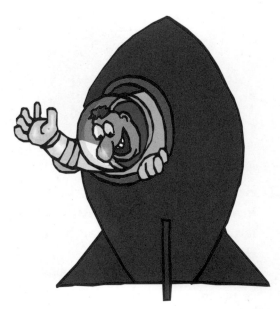

The word *good-bye* is a contraction of the phrase "God be with you" or "Good be with you."

The average American 14-year-old has a vocabulary of about 10,000 words. (In 1950, it was 25,000 words.)

Leathernecks is a nickname for the U.S. Marines. It comes from the high leather collars, called stocks, that were part of the early uniform of British marines. (Stocks were designed to force marines to keep their chins up.)

AEIOU
HKLMNPW

The Hawaiian alphabet has only 12 letters—5 vowels and 7 consonants.

Hoosegow is a slang term meaning "jail." It comes from *juzgado,* a Mexican-Spanish word that means "judge."

Famous Folks

In 1930, Sinclair Lewis became the first American to win the Nobel Prize for Literature. He wrote a number of famous novels, including *Main Street*, *Babbitt*, *Arrowsmith*, and *Dodsworth*.

In 1849, Elizabeth Blackwell became the first woman to graduate from a U.S. medical school (ranking first in her class), and the first female doctor of medicine.

One of the many sayings that Benjamin Franklin wrote for his *Poor Richard's Almanack* of 1733 was this: "The heart of a fool is in his mouth, but the mouth of a wise man is in his heart."

U.S. naval hero John Paul Jones was only 21 when he became captain of his own ship.

During World War II, Princess Elizabeth (now queen of England) wanted to contribute to the war effort. She did so by repairing military vehicles.

Henry Wadsworth Longfellow, who wrote *The Song of Hiawatha* and other famous poems, was one of the first people in the U.S. to have indoor plumbing.

Journalist Nellie Bly is famous for her record-setting around-the-world trip, which she accomplished in 72 days, 6 hours, 11 minutes, and 14 seconds in 1889.

Harry Houdini, considered America's greatest magician and illusionist, claimed that he was born in Appleton, Wisconsin. He did grow up there, but his real birthplace was Budapest, Hungary.

ANIMAL ANTICS

Celestial, comet, and lionhead are all breeds of goldfish.

To keep out sand, the camel has three eyelids per eye. One of the three eyelids is very thin. The other two have long, thick eyelashes. A camel also can close its nostrils.

Most calico cats are female. Only one out of every 3,000 calicos born is a male.

A caterpillar's head has six eyes on each side. That is 12 total!

The giraffe and the okapi are the only two animals in the family Giraffidae. Both live in Africa—okapis in the central rain forests, giraffes in open grassland areas.

A donkey has no trouble seeing where it is going. The position of its eyes allows it to see all four feet at the same time.

A hedgehog's heart beats 190 times per minute. That is about two and a half times as fast as yours.

An ant can lift more than 20 times its own weight, and pull about 50 times its own weight.

You can tell the age of a mountain goat by counting the rings on its horns. The first ring develops about age two; another is added each spring.

Science Fair

Edwin Land, the inventor of Polaroid "instant" cameras, also invented polarized lenses, which prevent glare, for sunglasses.

In 1893, Whitcomb Judson was granted a patent for an invention that he called a "clasp locker"— the zipper.

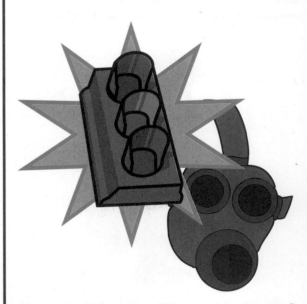

Explorer I was the first successful man-made satellite launched by the U.S. It was launched on January 31, 1958—four months after the world's first successful satellite, *Sputnik*, was launched by the Soviet Union.

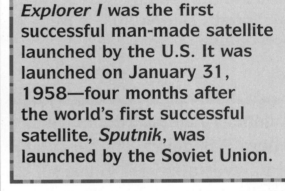

Garrett Augustus Morgan invented two life-saving devices: the gas mask (1916) and the traffic light (patented 1923).

The first practical lawn mower was invented in 1830.

A telescope on top of Mauna Kea in Hawaii is so powerful that it can see a penny-sized object more than five miles away!

A *nematologist (nem-uh-TAHL-uh-jist)* is a scientist who studies roundworms.

Dust from outer space—from meteors and other space bodies—falls to Earth, causing Earth's weight to increase by about 90 tons per day.

A *botanist* is a scientist who studies plants.

Nature Notes

Q. Which animal flies highest, the geoduck or the shelduck?

A. That is a trick question! The shelduck is a small member of the duck family. Like other ducks, it can fly. The geoduck, however, is a large member of the clam family. It can weigh up to eight pounds.

Q. The moon has no atmosphere. Does that make it warmer or colder than Earth?

A. Both. The side facing the sun gets very hot—about 250 degrees Fahrenheit. Without a "blanket" of atmosphere to hold in some of that heat, the temperature on the side facing away from the sun drops to -290 degrees Fahrenheit.

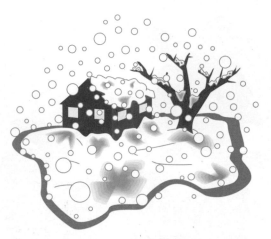

Q. When does a snowstorm become a blizzard?

A. When wind speed reaches at least 35 miles per hour, the temperature drops below 20 degrees Fahrenheit, and visibility is less that one quarter of a mile.

Q. What does it mean when someone calls a tree *deciduous* (*dih-SIH-juh-wus*)?

A. *Deciduous* trees shed all their leaves one season a year, then grow them back another. Maples and oaks are examples of deciduous trees. *Evergreen* trees, such as pines, have green leaves (needles) year-round.

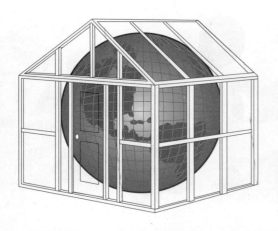

Q. **What is the greenhouse effect?**

A. when sunlight passes through Earth's atmosphere and its heat is trapped close to Earth's surface, raising the temperature

Q. **What is the difference between a nature reserve and a national park?**

A. Both are areas that have been set aside for the protection of the animals and/or plants that live there. However, national parks are open to the public, for people to visit and enjoy, while nature reserves are for wildlife only.

Q. **What type of flower is the world's smallest?**

A. the *Lemna*, also known as duck-weed, and the *Wolffia*, also known as watermeal (These tiny plants float on the surface of still water. The blossom is smaller than the head of a pin. The entire plant is only 1/16 inch to 1/8 inch across.)

Q. **What type of flower is the world's largest?**

A. *Rafflesia arnoldii*, also known as the monster flower, which grows in Malaysia (Its bloom can be a yard across and weigh 24 pounds. It also is the world's stinkiest flower. Its rotting-meat smell attracts flies the way sweet-scented flowers attract bees.)

THIS and THAT

In China, a bride wears red on her wedding day.

Since 1872, the official colors of Mardi Gras in New Orleans, Louisiana, have been purple, gold, and green.

In most displays and advertisements, the hands of a clock or watch are set at 10:10.

The largest cathedral in the world is the Cathedral Church of St. John the Divine in New York, New York.

48B98D12F

Pierre Lorillard IV invented a now-familiar type of formal clothing for the Autumn Ball of 1886. It was called a tuxedo—named for Tuxedo Park, New York, where the formal dance took place.

The Pluto Platter was the original name of Walter Frederick Morrison's invention, the Frisbee.

In 1847, Americans' average life span was 48 years. It rose to 65 years by 1947, and to 76.1 years by 1997. Experts think that it will reach 100 years or more by 2027.

The first auto manufacturer to offer seat belts was Nash, in 1950. They were an optional feature.

The Silver Buffalo Award is the highest honor given by the Boy Scouts of America.

ANIMAL ANTICS

Every day, a ruby-throated hummingbird must eat 100 percent of its body weight.

The average hen lays about five eggs per week.

The earliest ancestor of the horse was about the size of a modern-day fox. It was called *Eohippus,* or dawn horse.

Bees and wasps are responsible for more human deaths each year than poisonous snakes.

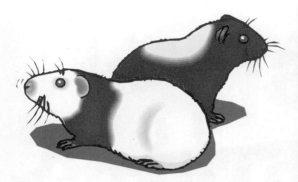

Of the roughly 4,660 groups of mammals, the largest is rodents. There are more than 2,050 known living species of them.

About 99.9 percent of all animal species that ever lived on Earth were extinct by the time humans first appeared.

The breed of dog most commonly used in search-and-rescue operations is the German shepherd.

The basking shark is the second-largest fish in the ocean. It can be up to 46 feet long (The whale shark is the largest.)

The giant panda is an endangered species. Fewer than 1,000 are left in the wild, mostly in China. Another 100 or so live in zoos around the world.

SPORTS STUFF

Nolan Ryan pitched more no-hitters and struck out more batters than any other pitcher in major-league baseball. In his 27-season career, Ryan pitched 7 no-hit games and struck out 5,714 batters.

The Little League was formed in 1939. At the time, it was for boys only.

No horse has ever won the Kentucky Derby two times—because the race is for three-year-old horses only.

Kareem Abdul-Jabbar scored the most career points in NBA basketball history: 38,387.

The very first Olympic Games, held in Greece in 776 B.C., consisted of only one event: a 210-yard race.

The same team won the first four championships of the WNBA—Women's National Basketball Association. From 1997, when the WNBA started, through 2000, the Houston Comets were the queens of the b-ball court!

In 1975, Frank Robinson became the first African American manager of a major-league baseball team— the Cleveland Indians.

The world's largest bowling center is in Japan.

The first televised basketball game was played at Madison Square Garden, in New York City, on February 28, 1940.

Science Fair

Q. What is tetrafluoroethylene resin?

A. The substance better known as Teflon. A chemist named Roy J. Plunkett discovered it in 1939. Teflon has an unusual property: One side clings fast to another surface (such as a metal cooking pan). Few things, however, will stick to its other side.

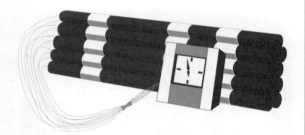

Q. What do dynamite and the Nobel Peace Prize have in common?

A. A man named Alfred Bernhard Nobel. Nobel invented dynamite in 1867. Nobel died in 1896. In his will, he left instructions for the establishment of prizes to honor great humanitarian, scientific, and literary achievements.

Q. What is *syzygy* (*SIH-zuh-jee*)?

A. *Syzygy* is when three bodies in the solar system—such as Earth, the moon, and the sun—lie in or close to a straight line. This happens twice a month, when the moon is new (its dark side faces Earth) and when it is full (completely lit).

Q. How fast does sound travel?

A. The speed of sound varies, depending on the altitude and on the temperature and density of the air it is traveling through. At sea level the speed of sound is about 761 miles per hour.

Q. What is Sedna?

A. A planetlike object orbiting the sun, discovered in 2003. Sedna is about 8 billion miles away from Earth and 84 billion miles from the sun. Sedna is so far out that it takes 10,500 Earth years for it to orbit the sun.

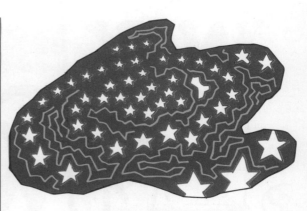

Q. Which star in our Milky Way galaxy is closest to Earth?

A. The sun. It is 92,980,000 miles away. Its light, which travels at 186,000 miles per hour, takes 8.3 minutes to reach Earth.

Q. What does it mean when a weather forecaster says, "It will be partly cloudy"?

A. It means that clouds will block out 35 to 65 percent of the sky. "Mostly clear" or "mostly sunny" means that only 12 to 25 percent is blocked, while "mostly cloudy" is 75 to 90 percent and "cloudy" is 90 to 100 percent blocked.

Q. What does a physicist study?

A. Physicists are scientists who study matter and energy, what they are made of, and how they behave and interact.

WAY BACK WHEN

Glass was first made in ancient Egypt, around 3500 B.C.

Susan B. Anthony was the first woman to appear on U.S. currency. Her portrait is on one-dollar coins issued by the U.S. Mint in 1979.

The world's first successful oil well was drilled in Pennsylvania in 1859.

The first shot of the American Revolution—known as "the shot heard 'round the world"—was fired at Lexington, Massachusetts, on April 19, 1775.